God of Wonder

Words of Inspiration for Everyday Living

To Kathy, on Blessings on your birthday! 7-8-18 Susan Jones Be Encouraged!

Susan Blackwell Jones

Our God is a "God of Wonder"!
(Psalm 8: 3-4) When I consider Your heavens, the work of Your fingers, the moon and the stars, which You have set in place, what is man that You are mindful of him, the son of man that you care for him?

SDC Publishing, LLC was established to promote and encourage aspiring writers and artists. It is a family oriented vehicle through which they can publish their work.

Contact SDC Publishing, LLC at
allenfmahon@gmail.com

Or on the web at SDCPublishingLLC.com

Susan Blackwell Jones

The poems herein are the thoughts and words of the author. Any similarity to other poems or prose is purely coincidental. All scripture references are from The Holy Bible, New International Version Copyright © 1973, 1978, 1984, by International Bible Study.

DEDICATION

To my Lord and Savior, Jesus Christ, who entrusted me with these words to be used for His Glory! What a Wonder!
This book is also dedicated to my family: Husband, Tom; Daughters, Erin (Jason) and Alison (Wayne); Grandchildren (Madison, Brayden, and Clara); my sister, Carolyn, as well as my many dear friends and life mentors.

CONTENTS

ACKNOWLEDGMENTS

I so appreciate the help and guidance of Al and Randee Mahon of SDC Publishing and my good friend, Rhonda McDonald.

Susan Blackwell Jones

GOD'S PRESENCE AND STRENGTH

(II Chronicles 16: 9) For the eyes of the LORD range throughout the earth to strengthen those whose hearts are fully committed to Him.

<u>HIS Presence</u>

Into HIS Presence
I want to come;
Falling to my knees
HE is my All---my sum!

In HIS Presence
I will praise HIS name;
Glory and honor
Only HE can claim!

Thanking HIM freely
For blessings bestowed;
Morning and evening
My companion on life's road.

In HIS Presence
I bow my face;
Overwhelmed and awed
By HIS Amazing GRACE!

In HIS Presence
Forgiveness I seek;
Humbly confessing
It is hard to speak.

In HIS Presence
My tears freely flow;
As I pray for obedience
And the courage to go!

In HIS Presence
I again realize;
HE will use my gifts
When I present them for
HIS eyes!

In HIS Presence
I am part of HIS story;
As I do my best
To tell of HIS Glory!

With HIS Presence
I can Trust in HIS STRENGTH;
HIS Spirit is within me
In every depth, width, or length!

(II Cor. 4:6-7; Ephesians 6)

GOD IS IN CONTROL

God created everything
And set the world in motion;
HIS power and might control
ALL THINGS
From the heavens down to the
Oceans!

When we read about these things
What need to fear and dread?
We must know GOD controls
All that lies ahead!

We are so amazed by learning about
The prophecies that have come true;
And we know in everything to come
GOD will see us through!!

Our minds cannot conceive
The precious ANCIENT OF DAYS;
Nor can we understand the
Height and depth of all HIS ways!

So we must put our trust
In GOD's strength and power;
Wait on the Lord and pray
HE will be there at the appointed
hour.

HE is ALPHA and OMEGA
HE is creator and guide;
HE will calm ALL fears
As HE walks by our side!

So let us step out and get busy
We have lots of work to do;
Our lives must reflect HIS GREATNESS
Until this age is through!

That's why we are here
To follow where HE leads;
HE can do the impossible
A servant's heart is what we need!!

Choose Joy?

Consider it all JOY---
How can that be;
When the trials I face
Bring me down on my knees?

How can I have JOY
When I look around;
In every corner of the world
Some trouble abounds?

How can I have JOY
When my heart aches;
And my soul yearns for rest
Do I have what it takes?

But you see, there is purpose
In all these things;
For in our weakness
We seek the strength God brings!

If life moved along
At a perfect pace;
We would rely on ourselves
And never seek HIS face!

When we remember HIS goodness
And HIS unfailing LOVE;
We begin to trust in answers
That only come from above!

It is not easy
To choose joy over despair;
For our trials won't end here
And life is not always fair!

I want to really learn
How to live as Christ;
Though HE chose the cross
HE knew JOY in the price!

I must tune my heart
To listen to HIS voice;
For happiness is uncertain
But JOY can be my choice!

(Nehemiah 8:10; Job 8:21)

Where Is My STRENGTH?

Father, I come to You
With eyes full of tears;
Trying hard to trust You
With all of my fears!

I lift up my prayers
For I am seeking You;
Life has many uncertainties
And I don't know what to do.

I will do as Jesus did
And whisper my prayer;
I know You have the answer
I know You are there!

I acknowledge my weakness
And know You can use it;
For it is then You can show
Strength's greatest secret.

You wait for me to stop
Trying to figure things out;
Relying on my own strength
I am filled with doubt!

When I finally give up
And let You take control;
I can rest in Your shelter
And let You set the goal!

When my path seems unclear
I don't have to walk it alone;
Your light illuminates the way
And Your Truth is shown!

God can use the little I offer
And multiply it into more;
My STRENGTH is found in Him
Surrender is what He is looking for!

(Daniel 10:19; Psalm 56:3; Pro. 3:5;
Psalm 28:7)

<u>"REST!"</u>

Father, I am so weary
And I know I need some REST;
Sometimes I'm overwhelmed
By the world's constant stress!

What prevents me from Resting?
Why do I commit to do more?
For when I am overextended
I'm depleted to the core!

When my Spiritual cup is empty
I cannot do Your will;
For my strength comes from You
And to You I must come to refill!

You have set aside a special time
Sanctified just for REST;
But I am often too distracted
My disobedience, I must confess.

REST is essential for my body
And for my Spiritual self, as well;
I am renewed by time with You, Lord
When in Your Presence, I dwell.

I cannot live without Your Word
Or survive without Your Love;
I must seek You daily, Lord
To have a relationship from Above!

You are my Protector, Lord
You are my Strength and Shield;
When I take time to REST
In obedience, I trust and yield!

Thank You Lord for Your watchcare
You created me and know me best;
For You desire to spend time with me
So I draw close to You and REST!

(Ex. 31:15; Ps. 91:1; Jer. 6:16; Mt. 11:28)

GOD, Are You There?

Father, There are times
When I feel so all alone;
I wonder if You're even there
Or if I'm just here on my own!

I fear when You feel absent
And I must face my trials;
I'm walking in the valley
On a path of endless miles!

But when I learn about You
And trust upon Your Word;
Your leaving me all alone
Is really quite absurd!

Your TRUTH is in a Promise
You would never leave or forsake;
No matter what my circumstances
This is a comfort I gladly take!

I know GOD is there
Without Him I would not exist;
He sustains me with HIS love
And by HIS Presence I persist!

I know GOD is there
When I pray a sincere prayer;
And answers come like miracles
HE rescues me from despair!

I know GOD is there
For it is HE who defines life;
The Joy of HIS Presence
Is a gift of great delight!

I know GOD is there
For HIS Spirit dwells in me;
For my heart knows HIS LOVE
And HIS Presence does not flee!

(Scripture TRUTH: Psalm 139; Job 38;
Psalm 5:3; Psalm 16:11; Psalm 66:18-19;
Jeremiah 23:23-24)

Open the Eyes of My Heart

Open the eyes of my heart, Lord
I need Your power and presence;
Let me remember Your promises
As I strive to be a woman of
Excellence!

Father, let me be reminded
Your words are written on my heart;
Each time I ask for forgiveness
Your mercy gives me a new start!

Oh Lord, it's easy to be brave
When I sit quietly in my chair;
But I need to feel you near me
When I scurry here and there!

Out there is the world
Its heart is not in tuned to You;
The battlefield is there daily
My heart must be renewed!

My purpose is to show the world
A different way to live;
But how can I show them strength
If I have nothing left to give?

YOU are my Power in weakness
YOU are by my side;
Daily I must seek YOU
To live with YOUR TRUTH inside!

Let my life be an example
To make a difference where I stand;
Let my heart obediently surrender
And joyfully take YOUR hand!
"Open The Eyes Of My HEART, Lord"

The Secret Life

I long to go to the "secret place"
Where distractions are at bay;
A special time for listening to God
A quiet place to pray.

I know I need the "secret place"
For here, I store up treasure;
The time I spend alone with God
Rewards me beyond measure.

My strength can only come from God
For I have no strength of my own;
In times of worry, doubt, or fear
I can trust in Him alone!

The "secret life" has benefits
That come through genuine seeking;
When I purposely set aside this time
I hear TRUTH that God is speaking!

Fasting from my selfish ways
Is a time for welcoming change;
The discipline of "giving up" control
Let's me examine what needs to be
rearranged!

Fasting means I'm letting go
Of fleshly things I do;
It centers my heart on God
So discipline is what I pursue!

As a Christian, I am called to be
A servant who gives to others;
In the "secret life" I freely give
Not trying to impress another!

When I tell someone I'll pray for them
I am sincere and follow through;
A card, a call, or even a smile
Are just a few things I can do!

I want my heart to be full
Of treasures I may not touch;
Like seeking to do God's will
And joyfully sharing much!

Father, I am counting on YOU
With Your Spirit my faith infuse;
So the result of the "secret life"
Will be a beautiful offering
YOU can use!

Based on "The Beatitudes" from
The Sermon on the Mount_-(Matthew 4:23-25)

Just BREATHE!

Good Morning, Dear Father
A new day has begun;
The birds are singing
Before the rise of the sun!

I take a deep breath
And let it out slow;
Precious time with YOU, LORD
Before my day presses GO!

This time is so necessary
Before chaos begins;
A few moments in Your Presence
And I can feel HOPE again!

YOU formed and created me
YOU know YOUR plans for me;
If I am to discover that
I must spend time on my knees.

In this uncertain world
I am being sifted like wheat;
YOU allow this , Father
To bring me humbly to YOUR feet!

YOU want to know who I am
And if my motives are pure;
So I need refining and testing
So my faith can endure!

I breathe in the fragrance
Of God's Holy Spirit;
Only when I am still
Can I rest and be near it!

Precious Savior, YOU knew
Right from the start;
I'd need some breathing room
To bring thanksgiving to my heart!

(Psalm 23; Ps. 91:1; Jer. 6:16; Matt. 11:28)

The STRENGTH

Dear God,
You are the **STRENGTH** of my heart;
And no matter what I encounter
You always stay and never depart!

What is this **STRENGTH**
That comes from up above;
That fills me with courage
And unfailing love?

It's a **STRENGTH** that comes
From knowing God cares;
And welcomes my questions
And any thoughts I share!

The **STRENGTH** that comes
When I'm at my weakest point;
For the Holy Spirit holds me up
With hands that anoint!

He rescues me
From Satan's schemes;
His **STRENGTH** pulls me up
His mercy redeems!

Our God has all **POWER**
Our God has all **STRENGTH**;
He knows every breath
Every depth, every length

His **STRENGTH** has created
His **STRENGTH** has repaired;
His **STRENGTH** has been patient
His **STRENGTH** has not despaired!

He ascended the highest mountain
He calmed the stormy seas;
He created every living thing
And conquered death for you and me!

The Promise: "In this world you will have
trouble. But take heart! I have overcome
the world." (John 16:33)

Thoughts of HOPE

How can I speak **HOPE**
Into my soul;
That will guide my steps
Towards a victorious goal?

HOPE comes from God
An assurance from HIM;
A light in the darkness
When life appears dim.

HOPE takes my eyes
Away from my trouble;
To focus on my obedience
With blessings that double!

HOPE is that feeling
Things will turn out for the best;
HOPE gives peace
When I need rest!

HOPE puts a song
Back in my heart;
And helps me keep going
When Satan throws darts!

HOPE keeps me focused
And helps me journey on;
It puts my feelings into actions
And turns my weak into strong!

HOPE helps me persevere
When I want to quit;
It can free me from strongholds
And pull me from the pit!

The WORD of GOD
Is where **HOPE** is found;
With "Spiritual Weapons"
That are trustworthy and sound!

I will follow God's direction
And with HIM, I can cope;
But I must consciously choose
Thoughts of **JOY** and **HOPE**!

(Psalm 42:5; Col. 1:27; Hebrews 6:19)

Susan Blackwell Jones

ASSURANCE OF GOD'S PLANS AND PROVISION

(Matthew 5:6) Blessed are those who hunger and thirst for righteousness; For they will be filled."

The Provision

Dear God,
Sometimes I am anxious
And grow weary in the day;
I cry, "Dear God, please help me"
I feel I've lost the way!

Yet you provide an answer
I feel it in my spirit;
You are nearby and listen
You speak and my heart hears it!

You make provision for me
My needs are daily met;
Somehow the way is shown
And reassurance is what I get!

I praise You for Your gifts
Blessings too great to count;
I glorify You, LORD
Your provision is like a fount!

I recall times in Your Word
You provided for others in need;
Like Moses in the basket

Floating among the reeds!

And there was a man named Jonah
Who said, "No", to what You asked;
Then You provided a "whale" of an answer
Till he was ready for the task!

Then let's not forget Elijah
Who asked You to show YOU are LORD;
So false gods would be shown as nothing
And Israel's faith would be restored.

YOU provided that day awesome proof
Baal was weak and doomed;
For when EVERYTHING was soaked wet
Your HOLY fire came down and consumed!!

Father, even in our doubt
YOU come to us again and again;
To show You will provide
If we will just trust Your hand!

You sent Jesus as our hope
His character above reproach;
Your Mercy and Grace are gifts
We only have to approach!

Susan Blackwell Jones

"The Unknown"

We just never know
What God has planned;
The things we fear and dread,
Are already in HIS hands!

HE knows our deepest thoughts
HE knows what's in our hearts;
HE knows what we need
BEFORE our need even starts!

Life isn't easy
There's a choice at every turn;
We can put our trust in GOD
Or focus on our concerns.

I am here to tell you
Satan will try to make you doubt;
He will try to steal your joy
And toss you all about!

But peace comes with knowing
We have a God with whom we can talk;
For CHRIST has already traveled
On the paths that we now walk!

There is comfort in knowing
HE faced every trial with grace;
For when HE prayed in earnest
HE saw GOD face to face!!

Oh, GOD, please help me see
What I should learn from this;
In my time of refining
It's lesson don't let me miss!

Thank you GOD for walking
On unknown roads today;
Guard each step and decision
As I walk the narrow way!

Thank GOD for a hope and a future
HE sees it laid before;
As HE gives me strength and courage
To arrive at heaven's door.

<u>Are You Ready?</u>

GOD is The CREATOR
HE does impossible things;
When GOD leads the way
Victories HE will bring!

Gideon was barely a believer
The weakest of the weak;
Imagine what HE can do with you
If you just walk in faith & seek!

Am I ready to follow Jesus?
No matter what it takes;
Am I alert to the changes
The Master wants to make?

Am I ready to let go
Of my own selfish pride;
Prepared to get on board
For this "Spiritual" ride?

I know I won't be perfect
Sometimes I'll get it wrong;
But GOD will use my weakness
HIS power will make me STRONG!

Am I ready to commit to GOD?
Even when it's not convenient;
My good intentions are lame
And with those GOD will not
be lenient.

Trusting GOD I will walk forward
With prayer and His Word before;
I'm on the battlefield for my LORD
With a heart that's been restored!

To read more about Gideon and how God can
use you, read Old Test. (Judges 6-8)

All We like Sheep

Sheep are defenseless animals
They need supervision;
They depend on the shepherd
For he is their provision!

Sheep have poor eyesight
And are prone to go astray;
They follow after other sheep
And ignore dangers on the way.

Moses and David were shepherds
They were being trained to lead;
Before they received God's call
HE knew the skills they would need!

God calls us HIS sheep
HE has The Shepherd's touch;
HE draws near to HIS flock
For, Oh, HE loves us so much!

The Shepherd leads us daily
On paths that are safe and secure;
HE watches every sheep
To be certain each step is sure.

HE gathers them together
At the end of every day;
In the sheep pen of safety
Where HE will rest and pray.

HE is THE DOOR of protection
As HE lays down at the gate;
The GOOD SHEPHERD is faithful
All night, HE will watch and wait!

Oh, how we need The Shepherd
Left behind is not a choice!
To stay alert to earthly dangers
We must know and heed HIS voice!

Jesus said, Very truly I tell you, **I AM THE GATE** for the sheep. (John 10:7)
Jesus said, **I AM THE GOOD SHEPHERD**. (John 10:11)

<u>Living the Right Way!</u>

Righteousness is trying to live
In an honest way;
Following God's precepts
Day by day.

It's setting an example
Of upright living;
Not selfishly striving
But with caring and giving!

Right Living is a choice
In what I do and say;
Seeking God's favor
Not the world's okay!

It's beginning to desire what God desires
And longing to live for HIM;
It's knowing HIS Word and following it
With His purpose as my guide, not a whim!

It's knowing what you believe
And living it out;
Being grounded in TRUTH
Instead of constantly in doubt!

Since we live in a dark world
That's lost its sight;
As a yielded vessel
We are called to live as shining lights!

There are so many people
Who are lost and alone;
Without any example
They can't change on their own!

We are called by God
To righteous living;
Christ showed us the way
Through His life of love and giving!

Right living is sharing HOPE
With a touch or a smile;
And showing others
Life can be full and worthwhile!

*Blessed are those who hunger and thirst
for righteousness, For they will be filled.
(Matthew 5:6)

Our Calling

We are each being used
By God every day;
Someone is watching
What we do and say!

Do our actions match
The words we speak?
Is it for HIS adoration
Not our own we seek?

We are all different
In what we're called to do;
That doesn't make me
More important than you!

Calling a friend or
Sending a card;
Taking a meal or
Mowing a yard.

Ministering in a prison or
Visiting a neighbor;
Watching a child or
Doing a favor.

We are all needed
To plant lots of seeds;
We live in a world
That's so full of needs!

HE will put on *your* heart
What HE wants *you* to do;
HIS strength and love
Will carry you through.

So whether you're speaking or
Singing, or visiting or praying;
Just make sure GOD leads
On the road you are taking!

My All

Dear God, You are so big
And I am so small;
Yet Your voice bids me
To answer Your call.

I do not always know
Where You want me to go;
But when I say, "Send me",
The way You will show!

When I try to take control
And rely on my pride;
I quickly lose the way
Without You as my guide.

For just like the Israelites
Wandered the desert 40 years;
I turn back to my strongholds
To find disappointment and tears.

You always have purpose
For each step I take;
And wherever You place me,
I know it's no mistake.

Each moment You know
When I'll stumble or fall;
But Your strength is my assurance
When victory demands my all!

Controlled by my flesh
I'll struggle to survive;
But controlled by You GOD
YOUR Word is active and alive!

My soul craves to know more
About the GOD I serve;
The truth keeps me steady
When Satan throws me a curve

I take time to remember
How my faith has grown;
And praise YOU Sovereign Lord
For all the blessings YOU'VE shown!!

What is Your Life?

What is your life
That God knew your birth;
And made plans for you
Each day on this earth?

What is your life
That you would come to know HIM;
And let your heart be changed
Seeking His grace again and again?

What is your life
Without God's control?
For HE holds the answers
That will calm your soul.

What is your life
When trouble comes?
You persevere and cling to God
Where your strength comes from.

What is your life
When temptation winks;
And your only escape
Is to do what God thinks?

What is your life
When you meet worry and despair?
Your hope then is in God
For nothing else can compare.

What is your life
When you fear tomorrow?
God can fill you with peace
And erase all your sorrow.

What is your life
When your joy knows no bounds?
You must sing and praise God
From whom all blessings are found!

What is your life
Without God in the center?
We can know "Mercy Triumphs"
And into HIS gates we will enter!

For more read the New Testament Book of
James

<u>A Holy Vessel</u>

Our God is Holy
He is perfect and pure;
We praise His Majesty
For His Truths endure!

He calls us to become
A reflection of Him;
Desiring to live Holy and
Be lights to overcome dim!

How is it possible
For a sinner like me;
To live blameless and Holy
Acceptable and free?

Only with God's strength
Enabling my heart;
Listening to the Holy Spirit
Its wisdom to impart.

I must be willing
To yield to His voice;
Surrendering my will
With an intentional choice.

I must daily spend time
Seeking God's face;
Desiring to know Him more
And accepting His Grace.

I must make decisions
During times when I'm strong;
So I'm prepared in weakness
To avoid choices that are wrong.

I must stay alert
And be aware of sin's pull;
To keep my thoughts Holy
And my actions faithful!

I must guard my mind
In what I watch and read;
For even what is heard
Can plant the devil's seed.

Personal Holiness
Is not about me;
But about laying down my will
To "THE ONE" who set me free!
*Apart from God I cannot be Holy.

God Hears

Oh, what JOY when
A prayer is answered;
Oh, what BLESSING when
Anxious thoughts are stilled.

Oh, what PRAISE when
God shows HIS mercy;
Oh, what PEACE when
The promise is fulfilled!

Each time you pray
God hears your voice;
HE sees your confusion
And considers HIS choice.

HIS answer is always
The right one for you;
You will face times of challenge
Until your journey is through.

You will travel on roads
Of confusion and doubt;
But have times of detour
To sing, praise, and shout!

Your mind fills with questions
Faith is threatened and tested;
Put on the "Whole Armor of God"
In you His love is invested!

Your individual life
Is so important to HIM;
He does not make decisions
Based on good luck or whims!

Your life plays a role
In HIS "Divine Purpose and Plan";
HE has a vision for YOU
To become all that you can!

Susan Blackwell Jones

GOD'S POWER TO FIGHT THE ENEMY OR FACE A TRIAL

(Ephesians 6:10-11) Finally, be strong in the
Lord and in His mighty power.
Put on the full armor of God so that you can
take your stand against the devil's schemes.

<u>Sizing up the Enemy</u>

Do you know you have an enemy
Who wants to shake you up;
He wants to take your peace
And your life to interrupt!

He finds your every weakness
He causes confusion and doubt;
He wants to come against you
Until frustration makes you shout!

He prowls around the earth
Like a lion looking for prey;
He is very quiet and cunning
And waiting day by day!

He cannot be everywhere at once
He cannot read your mind;
He cannot perform miracles
But he can put you in a bind!

God's Word tells us it is Spiritual
Between forces of good and bad;
GOD fights for us in the Heavenlies
So we can win and not be had!

The battle is unavoidable
Satan has already devised a plan;
But he has limitations
And he's invisible to man.

That's why we underestimate him
We don't take time with God and pray;
We get lazy and become complacent
As he slips in with strategies to sway!

We must be more aware
So we can prepare for the fight;
Then get our weapons ready
To defend against him day or night!

The enemy is ready for attack
He wants to catch you unaware;
So BE READY and put your guard up
Study God's Word and be in PRAYER!

Read: (Ephesians 6:10-19)

The Helmet of SALVATION

Salvation is God saying,
"Come to me;
See this gift of forgiveness
That's given to you free".

"Your sin is now covered
By the Savior, I sent;
All you have to do
Is accept and repent"

Now a new goal is planted
Down deep in your heart;
Your desire is Christ-centered
And you have a new start!

As you grow in God's Word
And apply what you've learned;
Restoration and protection
Are Salvation's benefits you earn

Salvation is a shield
That protects your mind;
From being filled with thoughts
That distract and bind!

The devil doesn't want you to know
In Christ, your identity is sure;
It is a fortifying weapon
And your inheritance is secure!

Salvation is hope
A confidence in God alone;
To walk with you through trials
Until you reach Heaven's throne!

Jesus Christ is your Savior
Salvation comes only through Him;
So set your mind on things above
And stop trying to please men!

The Belt of TRUTH

How do we know the difference
Between right and wrong;
Do we just follow after the world
Or trust ourselves to be strong?

Many people of this age
Say standards change with time;
So whatever goes today
Tomorrow may be sublime.

You just set your own rules
And go with what you feel;
And if it doesn't hurt anyone
Then what's the big deal?

The **BIG DEAL** is **GOD**
Whose Word tells the **TRUTH**;
He sets the commands in place
And HIS standards are time proof!

God never changes
And neither does what HE said;
Yesterday, today, and tomorrow
By this HIS saints are led!

Now the evil one would have us believe
We're being restricted and missing out;
That GOD is keeping something from us
His aim to invite questions and doubt!

God tells us to put on **The Belt of Truth**
For it gives stability to stand firm;
Then we have the strength
To avoid Satan's baited worm!

GOD'S TRUTH is a light
Shed on dark disguises;
So you can live in VICTORY
Without Satan's unwanted surprises!

Take every single choice you make
That comes to you today;
And bind it in GOD'S TRUTH
Then in HIS strength you will stay!

(Ephesians 6:10-19)

<u>Be Prepared!</u>

Lord, Help me dress
In the Armor of God;
For there are many pitfalls
On the road I trod.

When I accepted Christ
He pulled me out;
He cleaned me up
And set me about.

But the evil one delights
In making me fall;
He spends his days
Building detour walls!

But I can be prepared
For what lies ahead;
By utilizing the tools
God prepared instead.

I can live out righteousness
By what I think and do;
With wise choices
That have an Eternal view.

Prayer and God's Word
Are my greatest tools;
For the devil does not like
God's TRUTH or rules.

I can be bold in my actions
And choose what is right;
Strengthened by God's angels
Who for ME---fight!

We must pray for each other
With fervor and zest;
For strength and encouragement
To face each spiritual test!

I will be ready and willing
With God by my side;
When I utilize this armor
And with HIM abide!

The Shield of FAITH

FAITH begins
When first, we believe;
We cannot see it
It is planted like a seed.

It starts off small
And with time it grows;
God does not require more
Than simple FAITH shows.

FAITH is the way to salvation
As Jesus Christ, we trust;
He forgives all our sins
For He is faithful and just!

FAITH surrounds your heart
When you trust God more;
The Holy Spirit will help you
With whatever life has in store.

Our FAITH is a shield
That protects our heart;
From the evil that surrounds us
And Satan's intended darts.

But FAITH actually grows
When it is tested with strife;
For it is then we develop FAITH
That helps us stand strong in life!

FAITH is the intangible ingredient
That belief in God's Word requires;
For it is that very tested FAITH
That makes me tell of a POWER
that is higher!

Telling of HIS GLORY and all HE has
done is the goal of our FAITH!

<u>AWESOME GOD!</u>

The battle rages
Just over my head;
In POWER, GOD stands
And fights in my stead!

HE is not willing
To let any one of us go;
HE fights with TRUTH
And the enemy knows!

I know GOD is able
To conquer all adversity;
He wants me to win
So I see HIS love & mercy.

Each day I rise
To seek HIS will;
HIS power within me
Is ever present ever still!

The struggles and pressures
I face on this earth;
Are battles waged by Satan
To challenge my true worth.

I will not have victory
By writing my own story;
But only with God's help
And to HIM be the glory!

Oh how I am valued by HIM
Loved and cherished more;
Just so HE can rescue me
And share what Eternity has
In store!

Amazing GRACE . . . .
How sweet the sound;
My GOD is more than able
And in HIM, I am found!

(Ephesians 3:20-21)

A Better Broken

Bring all your broken pieces together
God can make them whole;
His light will shine through the cracks
And His glory will heal your soul!

No one chooses brokenness
We want a life of perfection;
But the very thing that pulls us down
Can result in "soul" introspection.

We just want the trial to be over
We want God to fix it now;
We grow impatient in the waiting
We ask "Why?" instead of "How?".

"Why?" invites doubt
And fills the heart with fear;
But "How?" changes our focus
So growth and change become clear.

We often are like the disciples
In our brokenness we don't understand;
We fail to see spiritual truths
In trials God gives with His hand!

Nothing comes to us
That God has not approved;
He knows the path of brokenness
Can be healed and then removed.

When trials come upon us
We pray and seek God more;
We are pushed to greater heights
That we would not have sought before!

When God doesn't fix things
A better broken occurs;
For out of our dark places
HIS GLORY in our hearts is stirred!

We are then inspired to tell others
When brokenness comes to call;
And that my friend is the purpose
Remembering God's faithfulness
through it all! (Psalm 40:1-3)

TROUBLE

Sometimes I encounter trouble
I didn't anticipate;
So I take it straight to God
And pray HE will investigate!

Sometimes my trials are small
And just need a quick fix;
And others are quite lengthy
Requiring a seasoned mix.

Whatever I am facing
I know God has a plan;
For HE uses everything
So much better than I can!

GOD purposes every trial
To root out my weeds;
So they can be pruned
And replaced with better seeds!

HE does not allow this to harm me
But to strengthen my trust in HIM;
For when I am in trouble
HIS presence is my anchor then!

I must keep my focus on the Savior
Instead of on what I face;
Like Peter stepping in the water
Had to trust Christ's saving grace!

When I keep my eyes on Christ
And not on the trouble;
I have HOPE for a solution
And peace amid the rubble!

None of us desires trouble
But each day seems to bring some;
And the lessons we learn on the journey
Cause great benefits to come!

(I Peter 4:12-13)

DETOUR

Did you have a dream
For how your life would go;
Are things running smoothly
Does your confidence show?

If you're like me
My path has changed;
In the detours of life
My plans have been rearranged!

We often map out
The way we expect to go;
But God has a better plan
HE wants to show!

Each one of us has a purpose
We might possibly miss;
If we go our own way
HIS plans we might dismiss!

We tend to linger
In "comfort zone" land;
But a detour from that
Challenges us to trust God's hand.

We see only in part
But God sees the whole;
We focus on today
But God has a long-range goal!

With each step we take
Our journey unfolds;
Submitting to God's ways
Helps us live our faith bold!

Sometimes detours
Help us discover unexpected treasures;
And in our struggle to trust Him
HE gives us blessings beyond measure!

(Jeremiah 29:11)

<u>Facing the Storm</u>

Paul knew a lot about
The storms of life;
When he accepted God's call
He experienced joy and strife.

Joy in seeing people
Accept God's Word;
Strife from others
Who refused what they heard!

Paul knew his strength
Was from GOD alone;
He knew his steps could falter
With the throw of a stone!

There are all kinds of storms
That may come our way;
What kind of storm
Are you facing today?

Sometimes storms come
From Satan himself;
So our attentions will be focused
On comfort, power, or wealth.

We choose storms of rebellion
When we think we know best;
And sometimes God ordains them
For HIS glory and our test!

Storms may come
Through another's choice;
We are left feeling helpless
Because we had no voice.

No matter the storms
That are headed your way;
Make sure God is your anchor
He never leaves, but always stays!

Don't wait until tomorrow
To make your preparations;
Put your trust in "THE ROCK"
And you'll have no hesitations!

For more about Paul's adventures, see
The New Testament book of Acts and
Paul's letters to the churches he visited.

The Confidence

Father, there are trials
In this life so hard;
Answers seem distant
And my confidence is jarred!

Do I trust You, God
To guide my life right;
Or am I trying to hold on
And control with all my might?

Do I really believe
You can work things out for good;
Or am I confused by questions
Of things not understood?

How can I put my faith
In things not seen;
And know without doubt
You are Sovereign and King?

Now these are questions
Everybody asks;
But we pretend we have confidence
While keeping on our masks!

We don't want anyone
To see below the surface;
But our LORD, the creator
Knows every plan and purpose!

He sees each life He created
HE knows what we must go through;
He tells the Whole Truth
About ME and about YOU!

We stumble into God
For we know there's safety there;
HE will guide our steps
While we go through the Refiner's Fire!

HE knows what it will take
To perfect every flaw;
We just put our hand in HIS
Until we reflect the perfection HE saw!

Susan Blackwell Jones

RESOLVE AND DAILY DISCIPLINE IN SEEKING GOD FOR SPIRITUAL GROWTH

(Philippians 1:9-11) And this is my prayer: that your love may abound more and
more in knowledge and depth of insight, so that you may be able to discern what is best and may be pure and blameless until the day of Christ, filled with the fruit of righteousness that comes through Jesus Christ---- to the praise and glory of God!

"DIVINE" Expectation

Did you wonder this morning
If the sun would shine?
Did you know that you are
Depending upon **"The Divine"**?

There are so many things
You've grown accustomed to;
You forget they are Blessings
From **"The Divine"** to YOU!

Long ago recorded in scripture
Messengers came with signs;
Telling the one chosen to listen
To a WORD from **"The Divine"**!

Moses faced a burning bush
The VOICE he heard **"Divine"**;
He was forever changed that day
For God used him by HIS design!

Samuel visited Jesse
To choose the next king in line;
Though David was the youngest one
He was chosen by **"The Divine"**!

An angel appeared to Mary
She was given a miraculous sign;
"You will give birth to THE SAVIOR,
For YOU are chosen by **"The Divine"**!

How often do you wake up
With a **Divine Expectation**;
Each day when you meet with God
Do you pray with eager anticipation?

Be AMAZED by HIS Presence
Seek HIM and listen for HIS call;
And YOU will have **"Divine Expectation"**
For HE is THE CREATOR of it ALL!!

(Exodus 34:10; Isaiah 40:25-26; Hebrews
12:28-29)

<u>Where Is My HOPE?</u>

When life sends me down
A slippery slope;
Where do I find rest
Where is my **HOPE**?

My **HOPE** is not found
In people, places or things;
But in The God I trust
And the security HE brings!

HOPE is an expectation
That things will turn out okay;
When we accept God's in control
We follow HIS steps day by day!

HIS unchanging character
Is comfort to me;
HIS unfailing love
Is a daily guarantee!

When I have difficult days
HIS strength keeps me afloat;
For I would surely sink
If I had no **HOPE**!

Let GOD fill your heart with joy
And the peace that comes from
believing;
Then you will abound with **HOPE**
And the Holy Spirit receiving!
(Romans 15:13)

HOPE does not disappoint
Because God's love has been poured out;
HIS TRUTH fills our hearts
That's what **HOPE** is all about!
(Romans 5:5)

God's love is unconditional
HIS Presence always near;
HIS **HOPE** is a powerful promise
Trusting HIM will calm your fear!

(Hebrews 10:23; Colossians 1:27;
I Cor. 13:13)

Perseverance

Perseverance must finish
Its work in you;
So your faith will mature
And be complete and true.

It's that quality that's needed
So you don't give up;
And the hope that encourages
When you think you've had enough!

It's part of your journey
When patience must prevail,
For the end result is in the wait
And the process doesn't fail.

Consider a seed
Planted in the ground;
It must first spread its roots
Before the fruit can be found.

Think of the caterpillar
That eats and grows;
Then rests in its chrysalis
Until a beautiful butterfly shows!

A tiny little egg
Laid in a nest of thatch;
Mother bird waits patiently
For her babies to hatch.

Tight buds formed
On each branch in the fall;
Become the leaves for the trees
When spring's warm sun calls!

God knows what is needed
To form and refine you
For HE sees the precious "pearl"
you'll become-----
When HIS work is through!

Read in the New Testament Book of James
about perseverance and faith.

<u>Seeking God</u>

Dear Father, I am seeking You
And trying to know you more;
I need to meet you daily
Behind the secret door.

A place where there is quiet
A place where I can speak;
A place where I am listening
For it is YOU that I seek.

O Lord, I know you love me
More than I'll ever understand;
For you also seek me personally
My name is written on Your hand!

You wait for me patiently
To repent and surrender my all;
You examine my heart and mind
And prepare me for Your call!

God, You are High and Mighty
I praise Your Majesty;
You are Holy and Perfect
Yet You bend down to know me!!

You took the time to come to earth
And experience life as we do;
So when we pray for help
You truly understand
Because of all You went through!

The Bible contains TRUTH to believe
Your promises are written there;
Your character and words never change
Amazing Grace is what You share!

I will seek You with my whole heart
And wait to hear Your Voice;
You will reveal the plans you have for me
Your strength will give me courage to make
The right choice! (Psalm 46:10)

<u>Obstacles</u>

All along life's journey
I have thought to do my best;
But relying on myself
Doesn't stand up to life's tests!

Throughout our growing season
We develop habits and then fears;
Then they become the strongholds
That control us through the years!

But we do not recognize it
For it becomes the way we live;
Until one day God convicts us
And begins to sift us through HIS sieve.

We put up many barriers
Between ourselves and God;
Our attitudes become negative
And laziness kills our resolve.

We say we have no time
Or that we do not understand;
For sin has overtaken
As we've pushed away God's hand.

Pride in what "we have done"
Grows a self-centered man;
Then we justify our actions
And ignore God's clear commands!

What are the obstacles
That are getting in your way;
Of a close personal relationship
With **THE GOD** who brings your day?

Recognize GOD loves you
And forgives your every sin;
Then pray for HIS peace and presence
And HE will surely enter in!

(Deuteronomy 8:2;   James 1:22)

<u>To Live Is Christ</u>

Father God, I thank You
For Your Word and its truth;
Thank you for a faith
To believe without more proof.

Help me to gain wisdom
As I study in anticipation;
So I can share with others in
Confidence and not hesitation.

Forgive me for the times
I fail to do my best;
And help me even when I fall
To gain something in the test.

Help me to press on
Taking hold of Your plans for me;
Depending on Your strength
From time down on my knees.

Help me choose integrity
As I pursue and run my race;
And set a good example
So others will seek Your Grace!

Help me to use time wisely
And not waste it on idle chatter;
Or spend too much time on things
That will never really matter.

Give me an unselfish heart
To love You more and more;
And I will know without question
YOU brought me safely to the shore!

I want what I learn
To change me for HIS glory;
So I too can say, "To Live Is Christ"
Was written in my story!

Read about the Apostle Paul in the Acts.

"Pressing On"

Each day when I arise
I give praises to the LORD;
He gives me strength to "**press on**"
In my heart His Word is stored!

I remind myself of His character
His purpose for me good and pure;
Each step I take helps me "**press on**"
And with His Presence I endure!

Daily battles ensue
As I wait for what's coming next;
I grab the rope of FAITH
And look for God's "Holy text"!

I hope you don't think that's funny
For I look for GOD in ALL things;
I believe HE truly cares about me
And I'll see HIM in the answer
HE brings!

Many worries crowd my day
Sometimes life is not so hot;
Satan just wants me to give up
Well I say to him, "I WILL NOT"!

When I think I just can't take it
I hear GOD say, **"press on"**;
And soon I feel encouragement
By hearing the words of this song:

Jesus, Jesus, Jesus
You are here with us;
Jesus, Jesus, Jesus
In YOU I place my TRUST!

I fight against discouragement & defeat
I keep my eye on the goal ahead;
Instead of focusing on my fear
I focus on God's sufficiency instead!

JOY so unspeakable
Abundant LOVE so true;
Thanksgiving in the face of it all
Keep me **"pressing on"** until I'm through!

(Philippians 4:6-9; Romans 8:26-39)

"The Molding"

God is my Creator
HE is constantly molding me;
Shaping me into the person
HE desires for me to be.

HE sends me on paths
I might not want to take;
But HE allows these detours
For HIS glory and my sake!

GOD knows my way
HE knows each tomorrow;
I cannot experience joy
Until I first taste of sorrow!

I cannot know real calm
Without going through the storm;
Or learn to rely on HIS strength
Until my weaknesses form!

I will not appreciate gain
Until some loss has come my way;
Or have the blessings of obedience
Until self-will has had its day!

How can I learn about forgiveness
Until unforgiveness is gone;
Or experience HIS comfort
In times when fear is strong?

GOD surely works unexpectedly
His ways are not our ways;
HIS ministry was just like this
When on earth HE lived HIS days!

The poor will be rich
The weak will be strong;
The first will be last
The self-righteous will be wrong!

I have the HOPE of Eternal Life
When my time on earth will cease;
For it is only in HIS PRESENCE
I will experience HIS TRUE PEACE!

TO LOVE THE TRUTH

Oh GOD, who in tender mercy
Tests us all;
To determine our hearts
So we will not fall!

Who desires for HIS people
To know LOVE and TRUTH;
But more than that
YOU want us to live it as proof!

Proof that we know
And honor YOUR teachings;
Proof that we remember
YOUR LOVE is far-reaching!

To know YOU pursue us
And patiently wait;
While we live our lives
YOUR return will not be late!

The world is turning
From YOUR TRUTH to an illusion;
And one day it will awaken
To see Satan's hidden delusion!

To LOVE the TRUTH
And not be deceived;
Reveals our Belief in YOU
Has by FAITH been received!

To LOVE the TRUTH
Guides choices of behavior;
To LOVE the TRUTH
Is to LOVE the SAVIOUR!

Open our eyes, LORD
To see paths of RIGHT;
For the GLORY of JESUS
Turns all darkness to LIGHT!

For more, read the New Testament
Books of I & II Thessalonians.

<u>What Are You Eating?</u>

When I accepted Jesus
As my personal Savior;
I saw things differently
It changed my behavior!

I knew the basics
The "milk" of The Word;
And I listened and learned
From all that I heard.

I memorized a few verses
That were foundation stones;
But I knew I needed more
To make my faith my own.

I needed more than "milk"
To develop and grow;
I craved deeper understanding
Before maturity would show.

That is the way
For all new believers;
You must have the "meat"
To withstand Satan's deceivers.

Paul offered the Corinthians "milk"
For the "meat" they were not ready;
They were worldly and immature
And not yet "spiritually steady"!

Still relying on and following
Their old way of life;
Filled with jealousy and quarreling
Distraction and strife!

So what can you say
About <u>YOUR</u> spiritual heart;
Are you making progress
Are you partaking in the "meat part"?

Have you moved beyond
What all God can do for you;
And developed HIS character
By doing what HE planned for you?

What might be keeping you
From moving ahead;
You know "Faith without works
Is already dead"!

Grow deep roots in Christ
And remember your story;
Tell it to others
And give HIM all the glory!

THE HEALING OF FORGIVENESS

(II Chronicles 7:14: If My people, who are called by My name, will humble themselves and pray and seek My face and turn from their wicked ways, then will I hear from heaven and will forgive their sin and heal their land.)

The Stone of Unforgiveness

Someone gave me a stone
And said, "Do not hold it tight";
For it represents unforgiveness
We hold onto with all our might!

The stone was rough and jagged
Its edges were not smooth,
And the same can happen to us
If we allow our heart to be unmoved.

Our attitude about forgiveness
Can cause resentment you see;
For we feel justified in our anger
We become imprisoned and not free!

When we do not forgive
And refuse to let it go,
The one who has wronged us
Doesn't care and doesn't know!

The elements of the "offense"
Which caused such anguish and tears,
Begins to change and mold <u>US</u>
Like the stone throughout the years.

We must give our hurts to God
Forgive and let them go,
Then healing can begin
And HE will start to help us grow.

Now the "stone" of "unforgiveness"
Still rests within **MY** hand,
And I must make the choice
Keep it ---OR--- throw it in the sand!

I will do as **GOD** asks
I am ready to be set free!
For if I will not forgive my brother
God cannot forgive me.

What about you? Are you holding on
to unforgiveness? Will you throw your
"stone" to the ground? (Colossians 3:13)

The Peace Of Forgiveness

What is forgiveness?
How does it begin?
It starts when I recognize
My disobedience is sin.

I must go to God
And confess my mistake;
Christ's blood is my covering
He died for my sake!

Now relationship is restored
His forgiveness sets me free;
The debt has been paid
For you and for me!

The same must occur
Between those who disagree;
To set aside differences
If mending is to be.

God's word commands
We must learn to forgive;
Restoration and harmony
Is how He wants us to live.

Forgiveness is not easy
Someone must take the first step;
Pray before having conversation
To have honesty and depth.

So don't hold a grudge
Or refuse an apology;
Forgive as you are forgiven
And peace you will see.

The act of forgiveness
Is finally letting go;
Of bitterness and anger
So God's love can show.
*Who do <u>YOU</u> need to forgive?"

Concealed

We all have things
We have tried to conceal;
They are hidden inside
They don't even feel real.

We've never faced truth
Where the issue is concerned;
So it just settled down deep
Like a slow simmering burn!

Then one day we are confronted
To face our deepest fear;
And we are freed from within
For we know Christ is near!

Now healing can begin
The chains are finally broken;
Surrounded by love
The concealed can be spoken!

As long as we hold on
To our guilt and blame;
The devil will use it
To grow fear and shame!

Oh God, Please forgive me
For holding on to hidden things;
Shine YOUR light in the darkness
With the healing peace it brings!

Whether you have done something
Or something has been done to you;
Christ has washed you clean
Now you can begin anew!

The GRACE

GRACE is unmerited favor
A gift so undeserved;
Yet if we will accept it
A place with Christ is reserved.

We can barely grasp its meaning
For we know not what to say;
To have all our sins covered
And our shame just taken away!

Such unbelievable forgiveness
And overwhelming love;
Can only come from perfection
In the GOD who dwells above!

The works we do on earth
Cannot earn this **GRACE**;
But are only a reflection
Of the Truth that we embrace.

We know about the awful things
That people choose to do;
But we are reminded again
GRACE covers the sins of me & you!

Through the blood of Jesus Christ
Our debt is paid in full;
His **GRACE** is sufficient
And more valuable than any jewel!

Oh to be so cherished
And by our faith be justified;
Then lavished with His **GRACE**
And with HIM safely abide!

The Promise: My GRACE is sufficient
for you, for my power is made perfect
in weakness. (II Corinthians 12:9)

<u>God at the Center</u>

LORD, how do I let YOU become
"The Center" of my thoughts;
And allow YOUR leading
To help me live as I ought?

To let YOU become <u>The Guide</u>
For the thoughts I seek;
And <u>The Guard </u>for my mouth
With the words I speak!

To let YOU become the standard
By which I measure my actions;
And keep me accountable
To avoid hasty reactions!

YOU have set the moral compass
Help me abide by YOUR Word;
And make all decisions through
Holy Spirit's voice I've heard.

O LORD, forgive me
For being full of myself;
When I see my thoughts and concerns
Sitting on my prayer shelf.

Let me hear YOUR TRUTH
Speaking to my heart;
And reform my attitude
To make a new start!

Help me be more grateful
For all YOU have done for me;
And to remember all YOUR benefits
So I can become a light for others to see.

LORD, Become the Center
Of my ever flowing thoughts;
And make me consciously aware
That in GOD'S hands, I am caught!

(Psalm 19:14; Psalm 103:2)

The Search

From the very beginning
In God's Perfect Creation;
Man has searched for more
And found only temptation!

The empty space within
Designed by the Creator;
Will never be filled
By the world's imitator!

His Perfect Love continually
Searches to draw me back;
To a place of communion
Where His forgiveness has no lack!

What love is this
That searches for me still;
Even when I go my own way
And instead do my will?

It's an Eternal Love
That seeks to save;
Unselfish, Unending
His whole life He gave!

Maybe God's love has come
Many times for you;
And you've grown complacent
With the message of good news.

Search again for The Christ
Renew your heart;
He searches for you still
He has done His part!

He can shower me with blessings
Or take it all away;
But when I follow Him
I will no longer search for The Way!

Read more about Jesus Christ in the New
Testament books of Matthew, Mark, Luke,
John

ABOUT THE AUTHOR

Susan Blackwell Jones was born and raised in the mountain state of West Virginia. Her life has been blessed with a loving and encouraging family, many dear friends and mentors whom God has placed along her journey.

She received an A.S Degree from Bluefield College and a B.S Degree in Elementary Education from Concord College.

Susan and husband Tom have been married 47 years and have two grown daughters and their husbands, and three grandchildren.

Living in Virginia, Susan taught first and second grades in public schools for 34 years, never imagining the new path God would lead her on in retirement.

A simple choice to go to a Bible Study at her church would result in her leading Wednesday Women Bible Study and the beginning of God's gifting her with these amazing poems.

Realizing more and more the need for people today to hear words of encouragement and hope, the poems have been a vehicle to begin conversations with others about Christ, express love and compassion to those in need, and to enhance spiritual growth through Bible Study and daily devotion.

Susan Blackwell Jones